Romantic Art Deco

a sexy adult coloring book

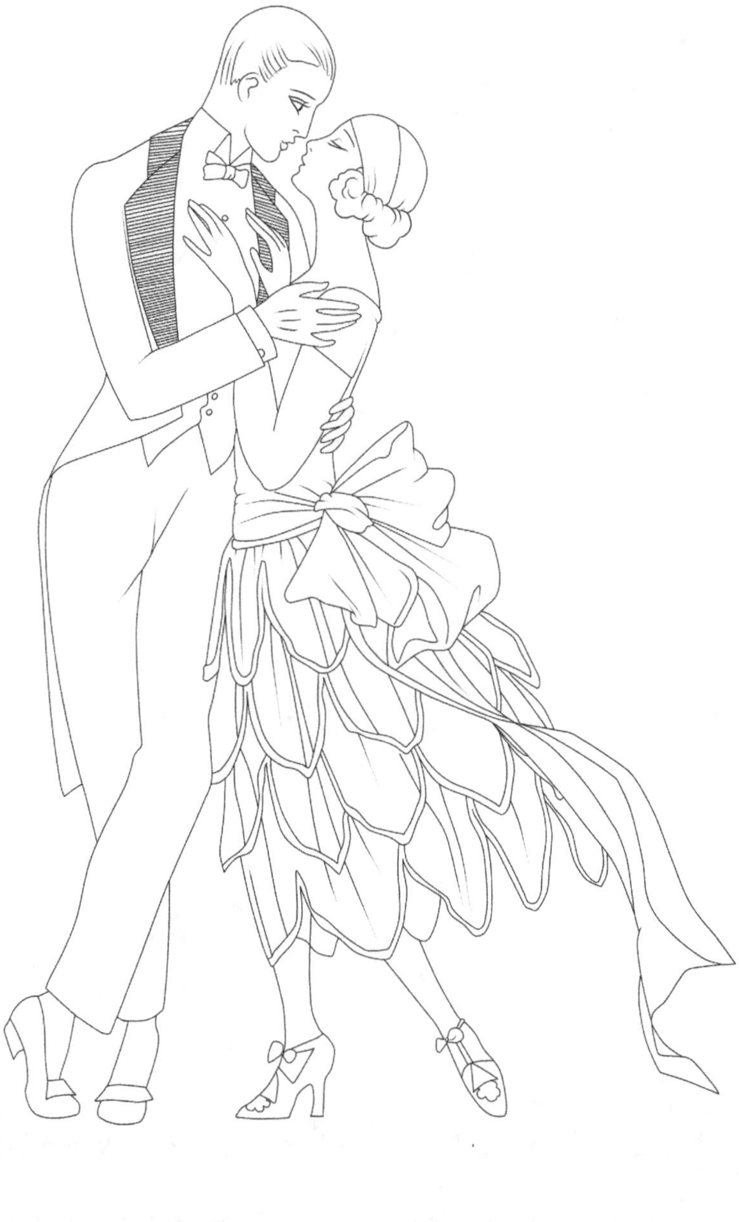

by Natalie Tate

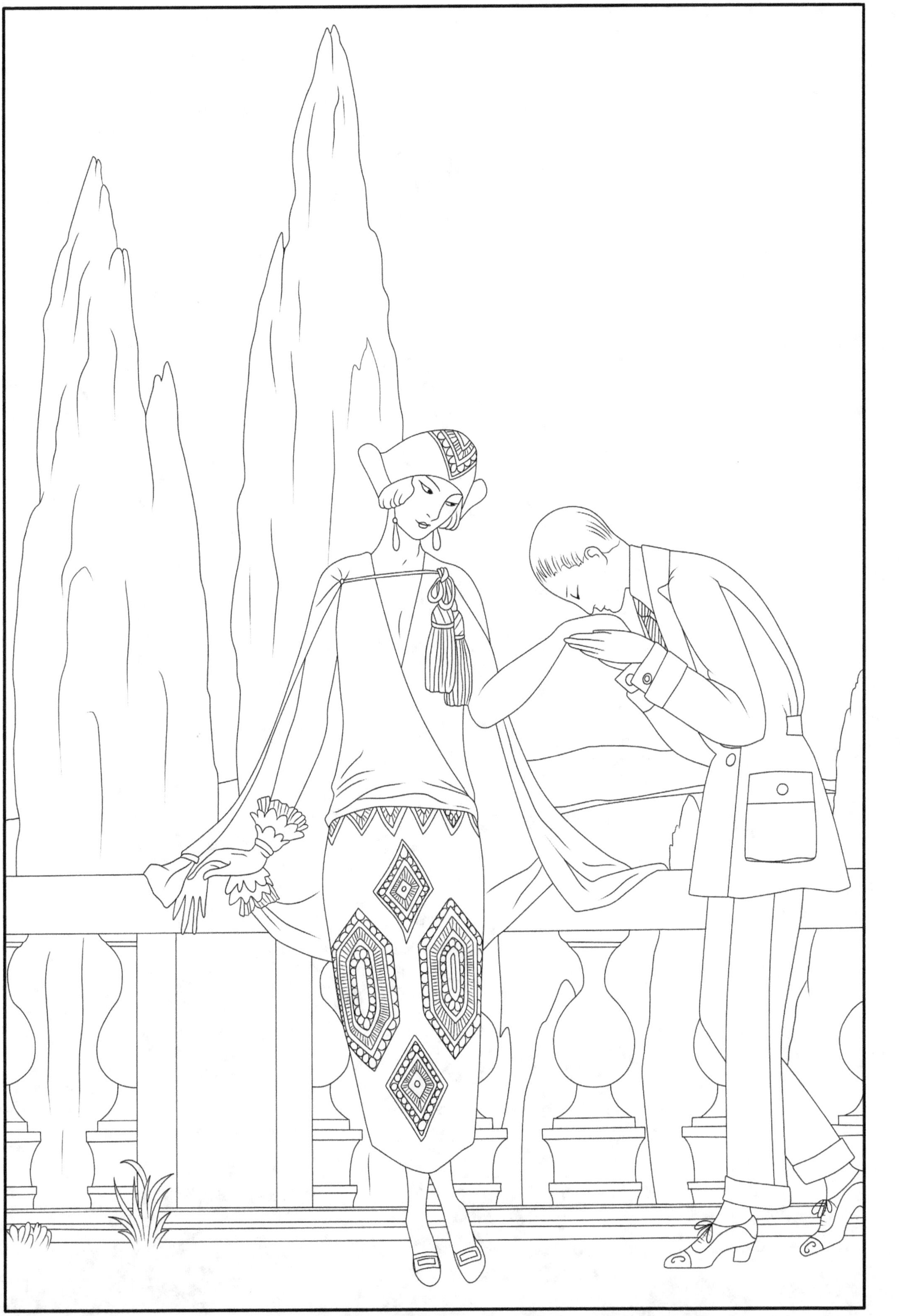

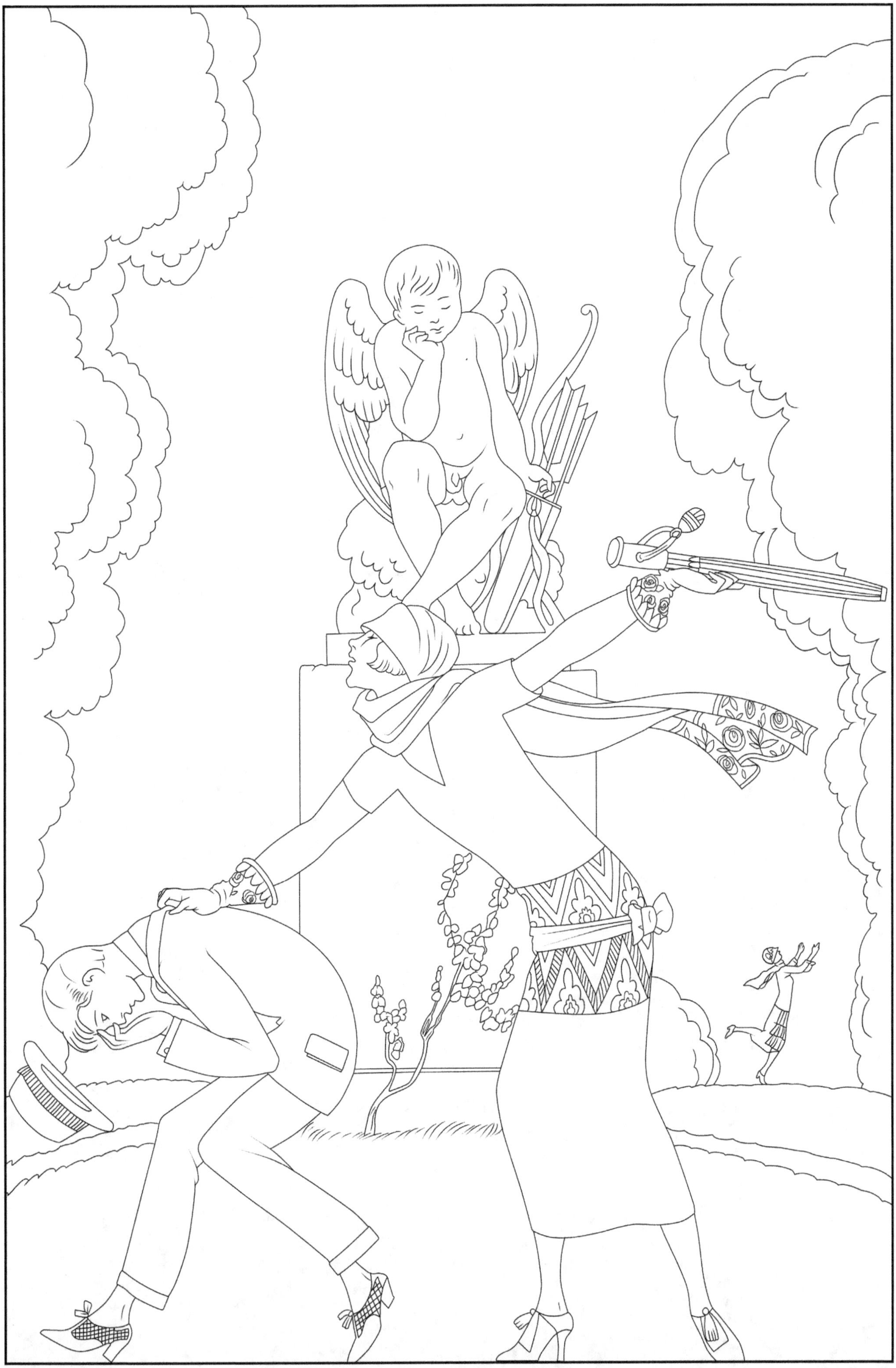

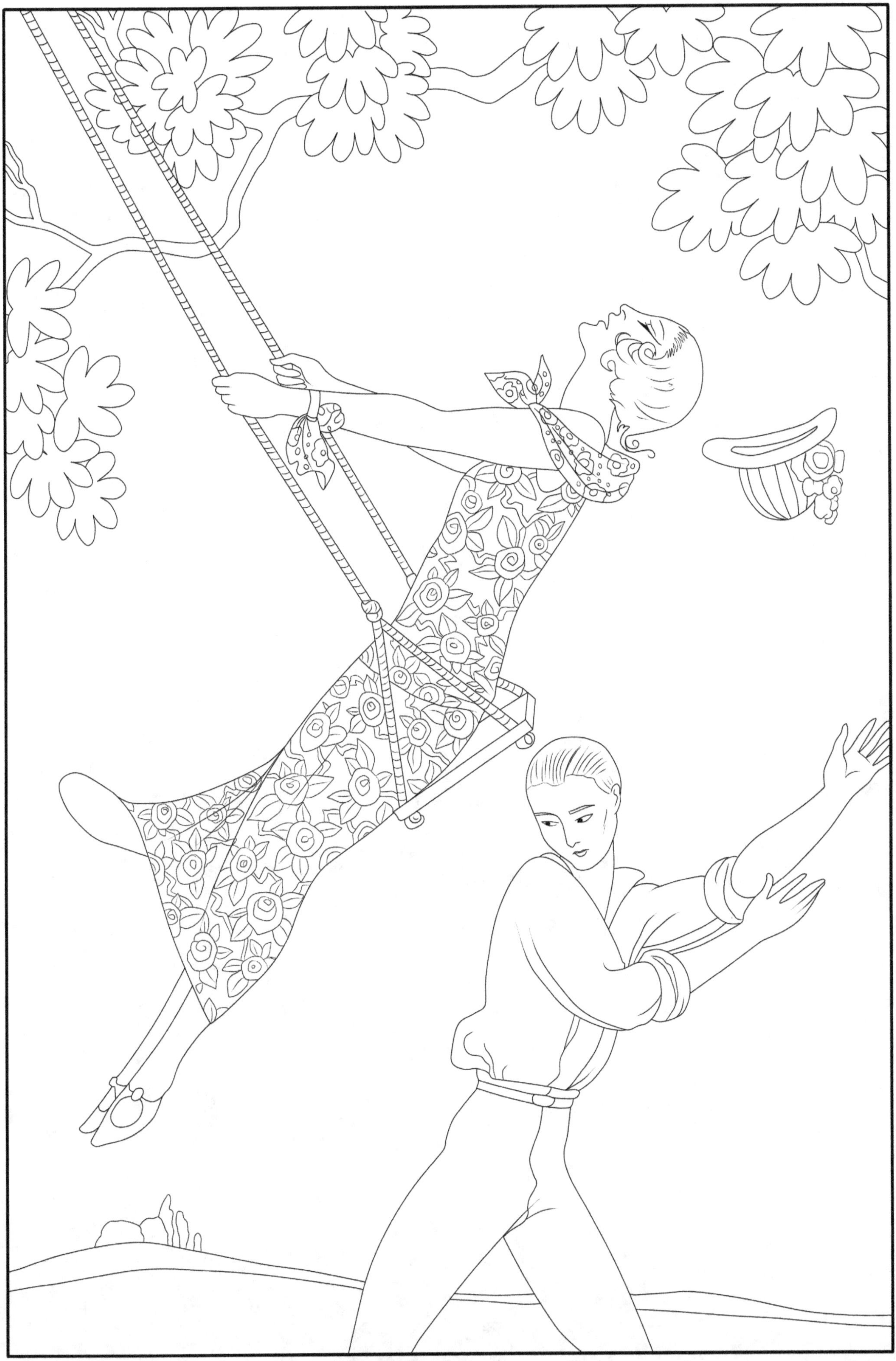

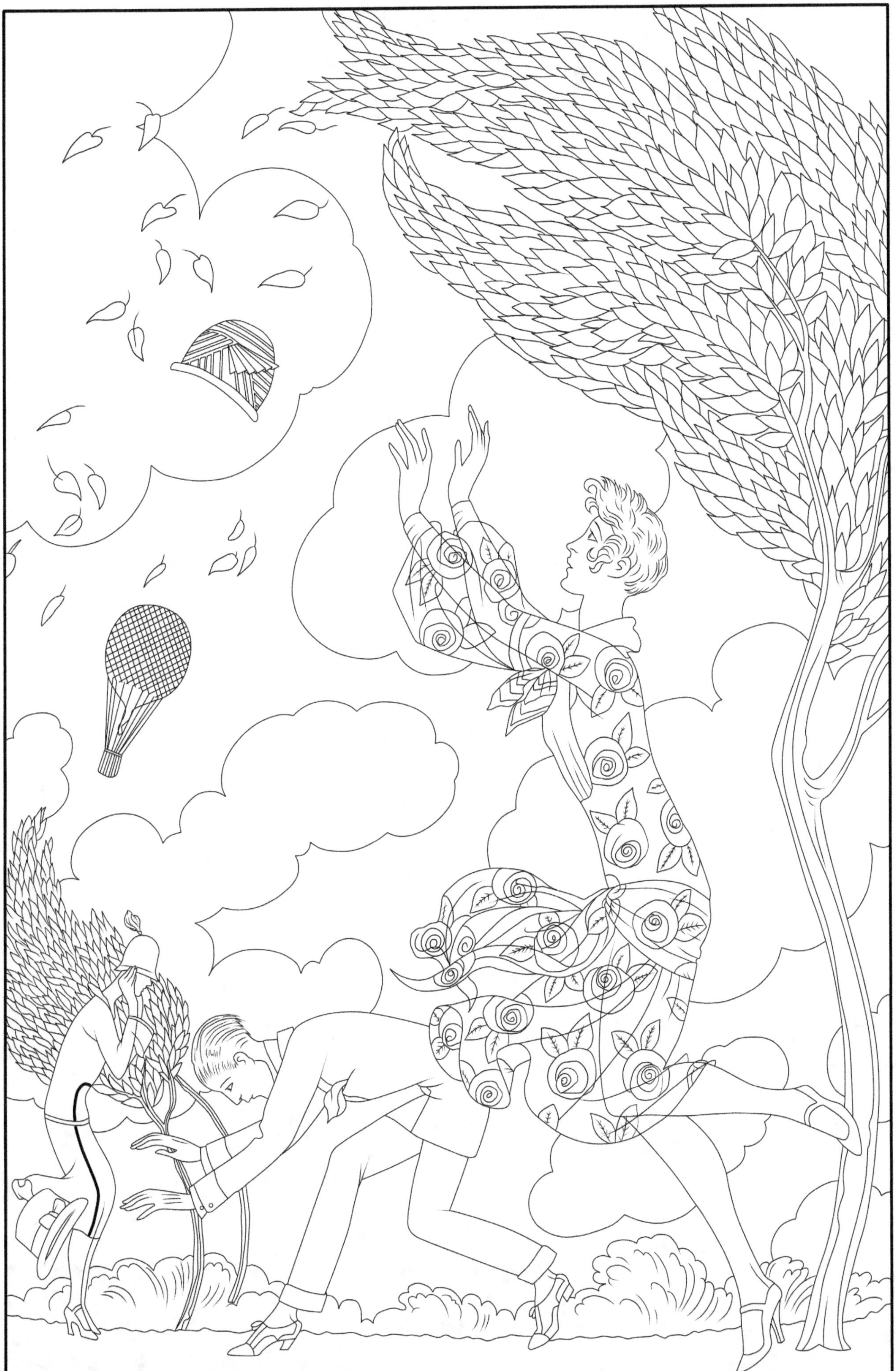

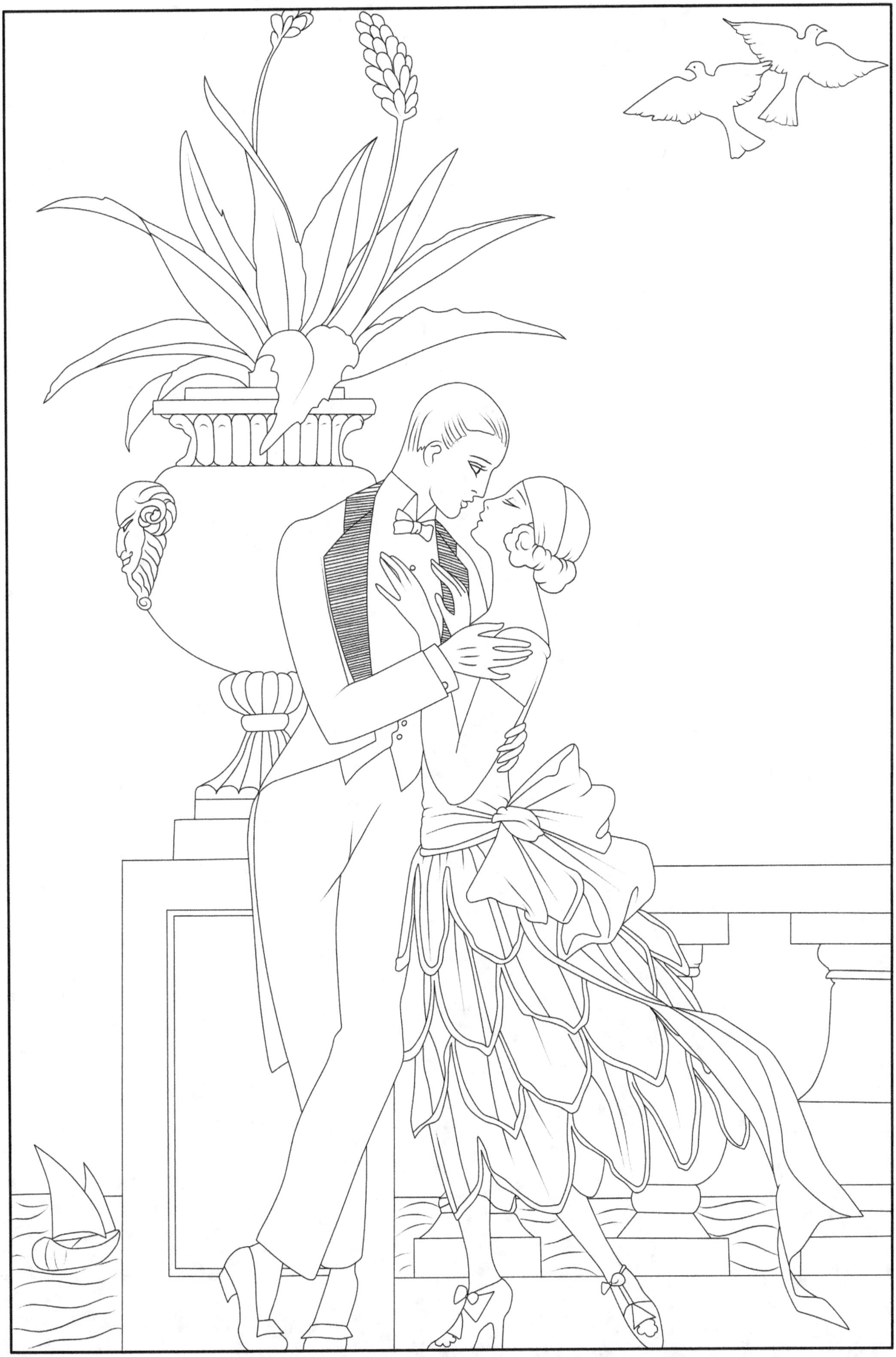

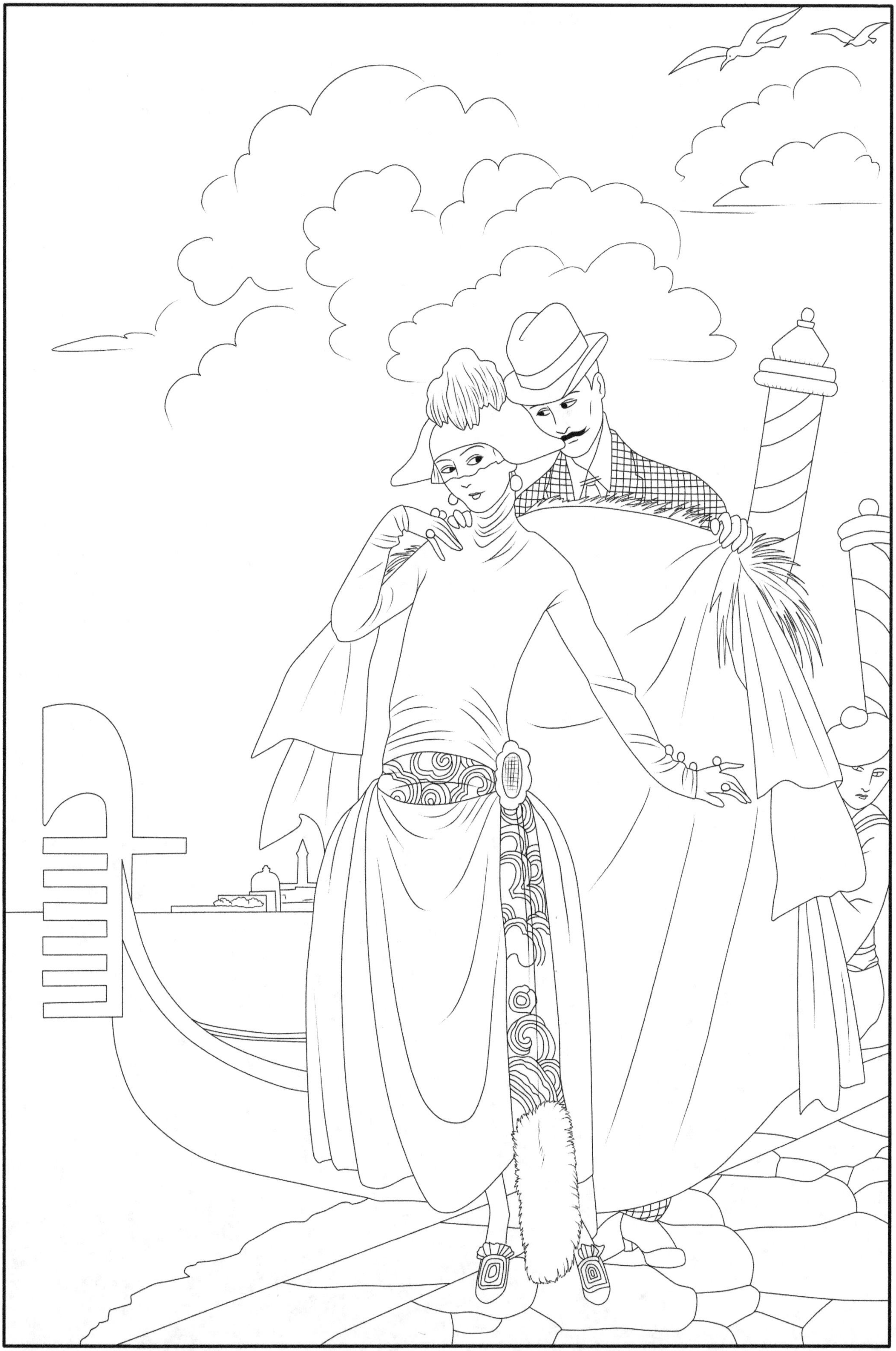

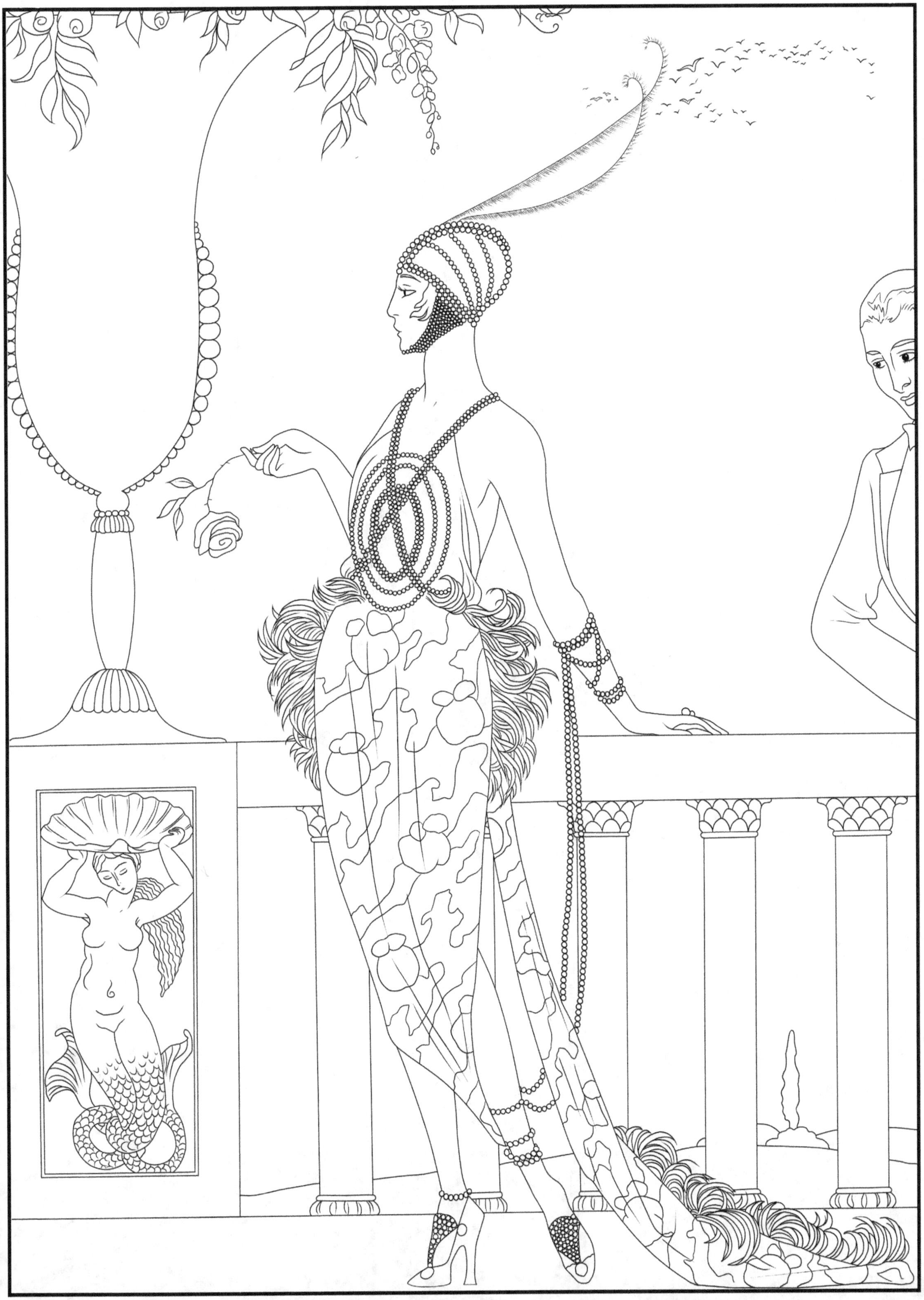

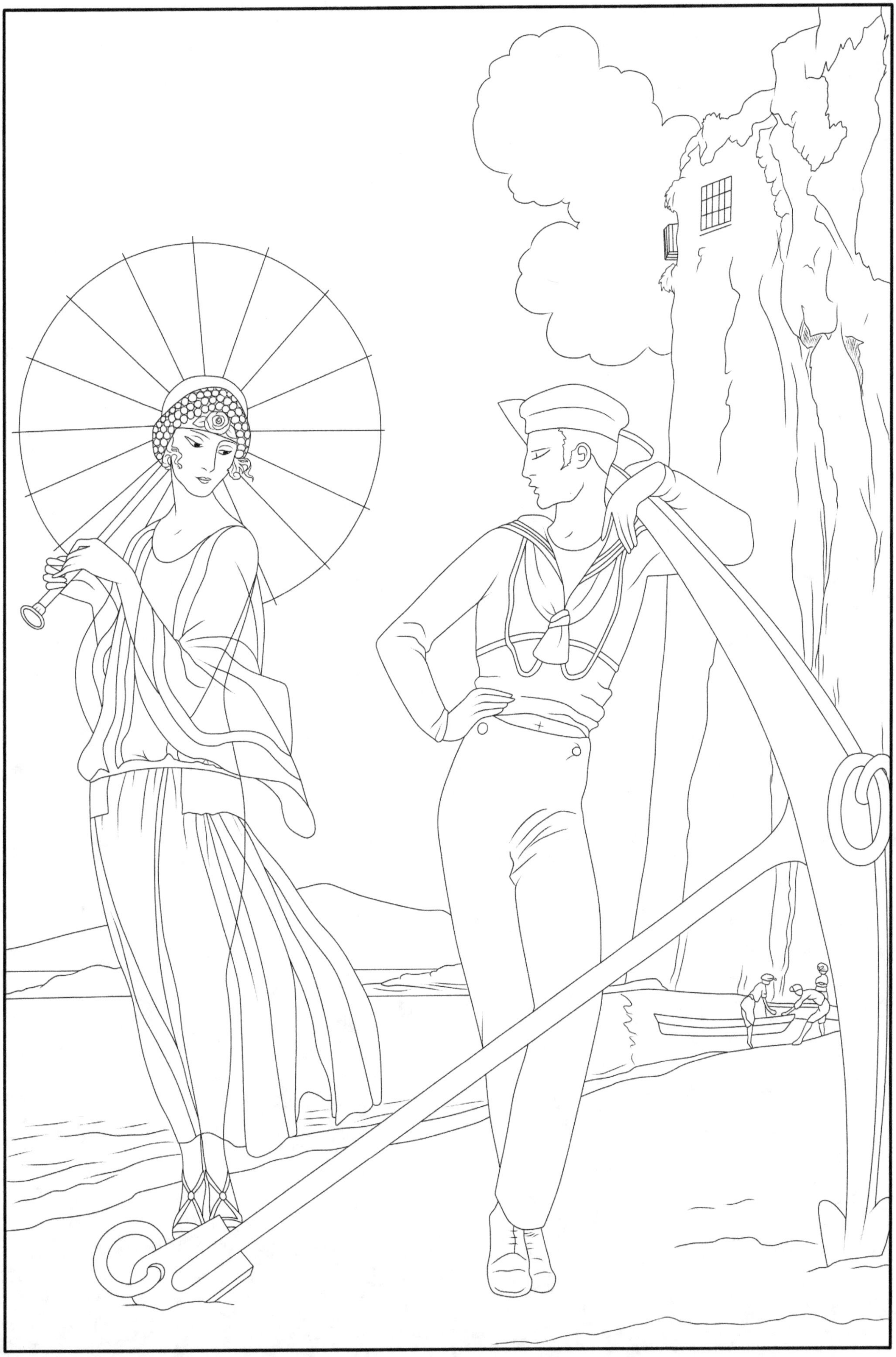

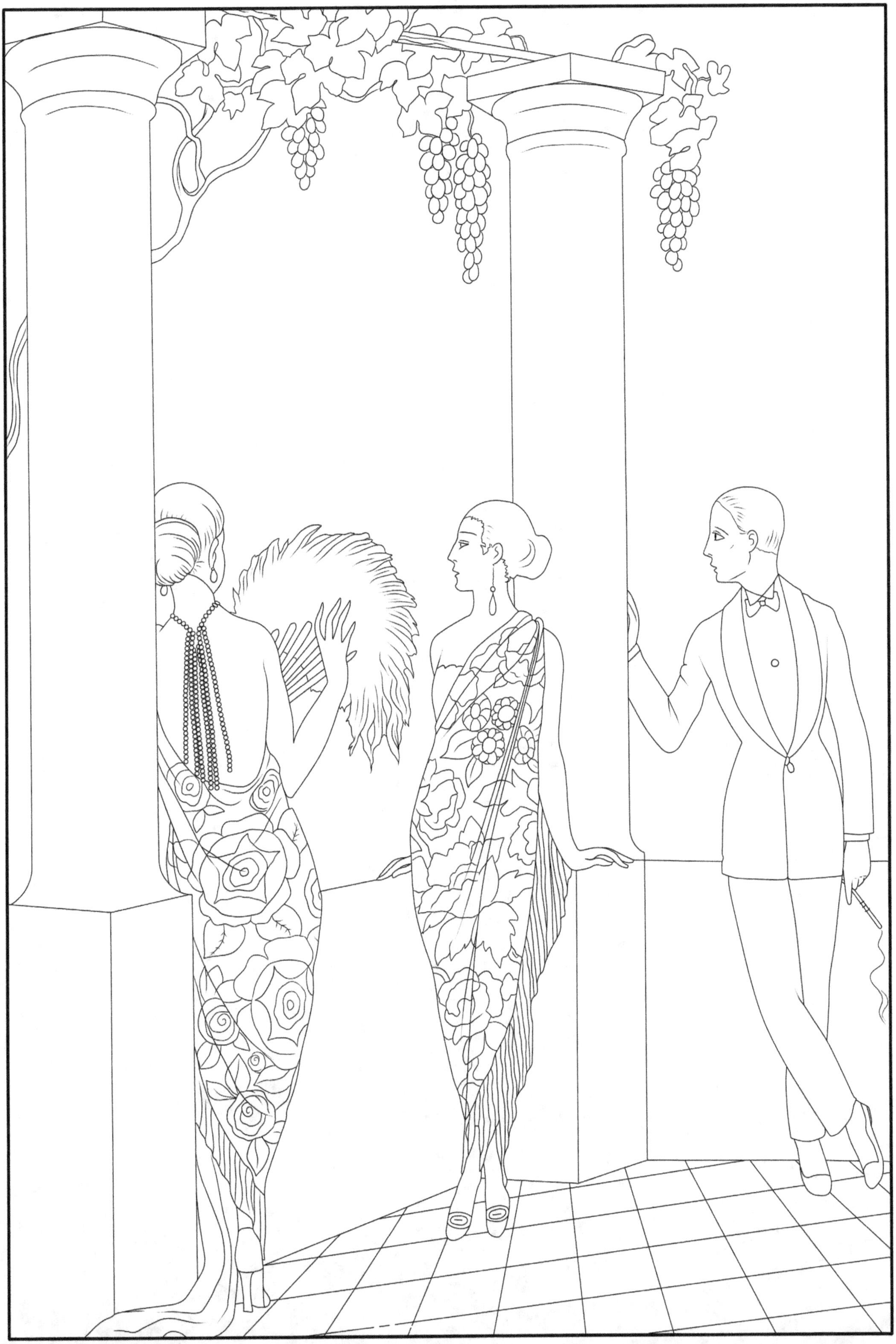

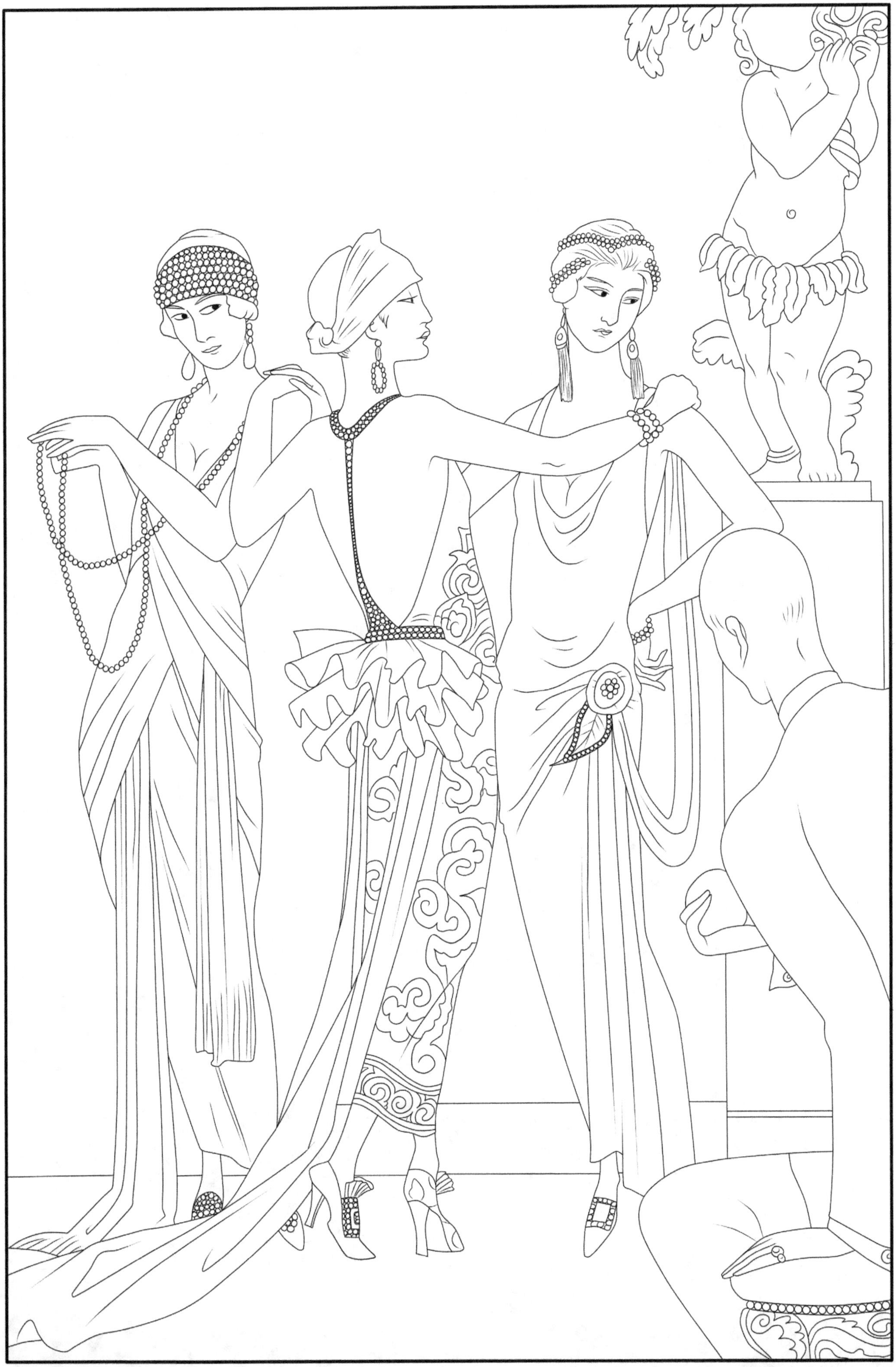

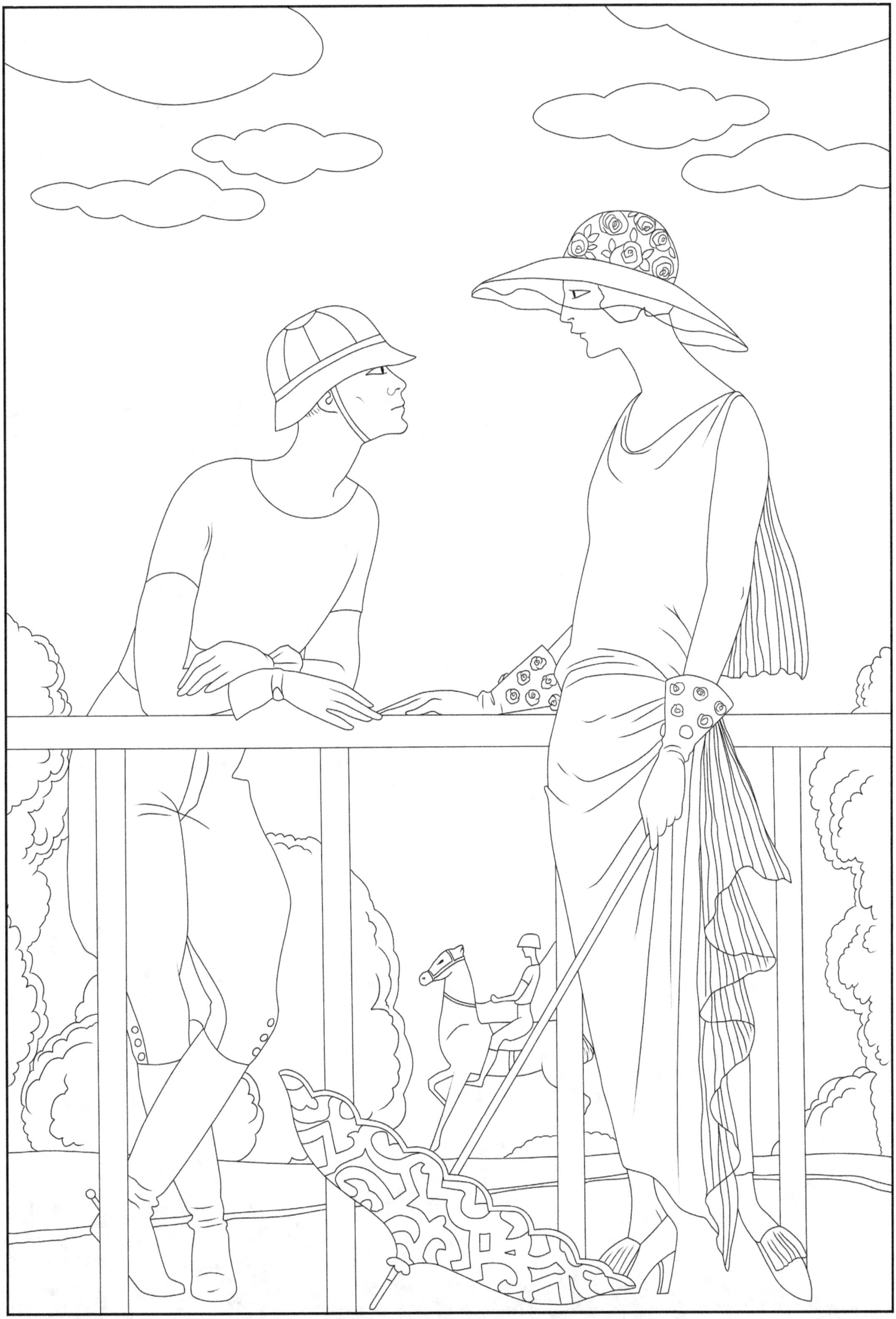

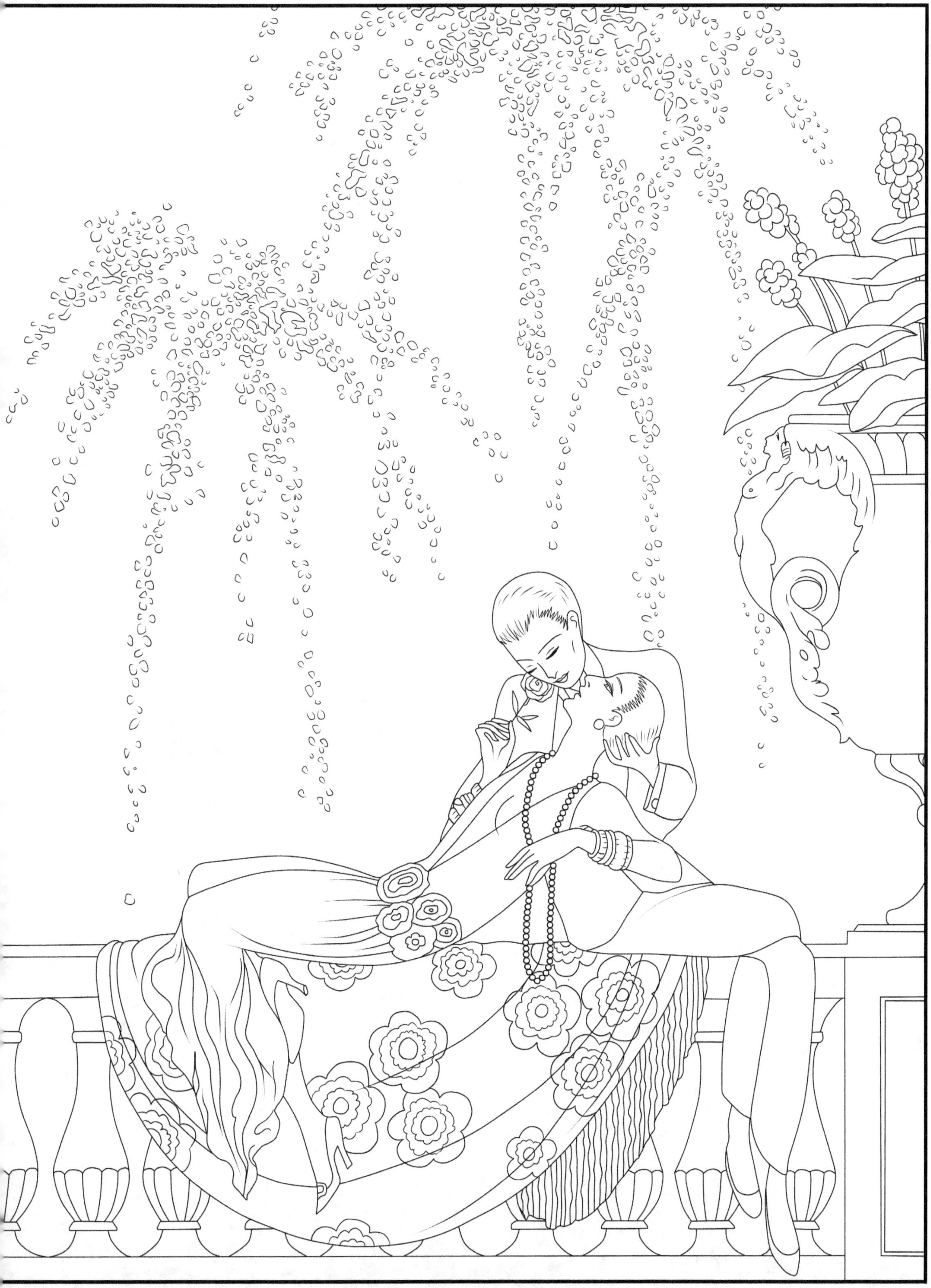

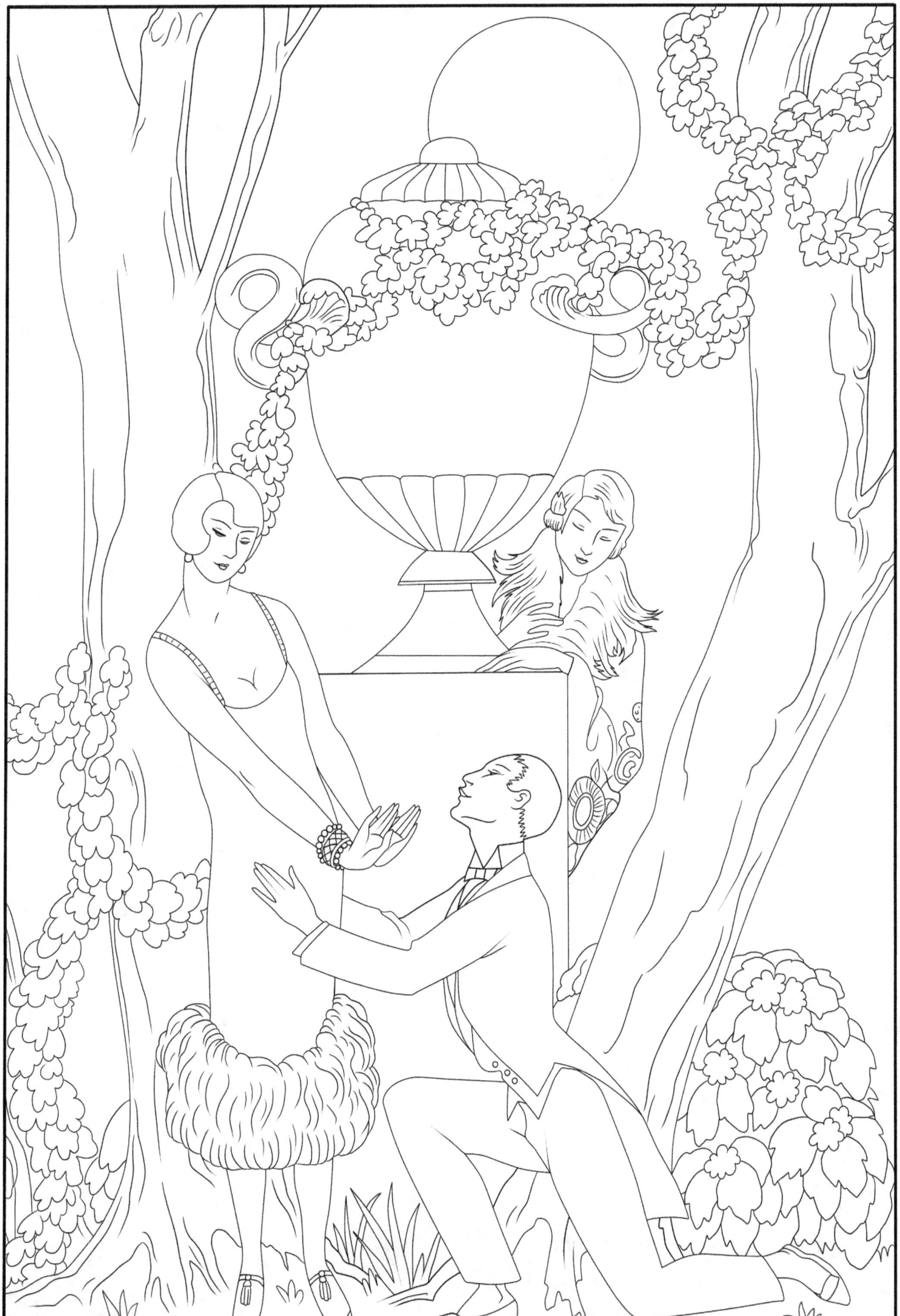

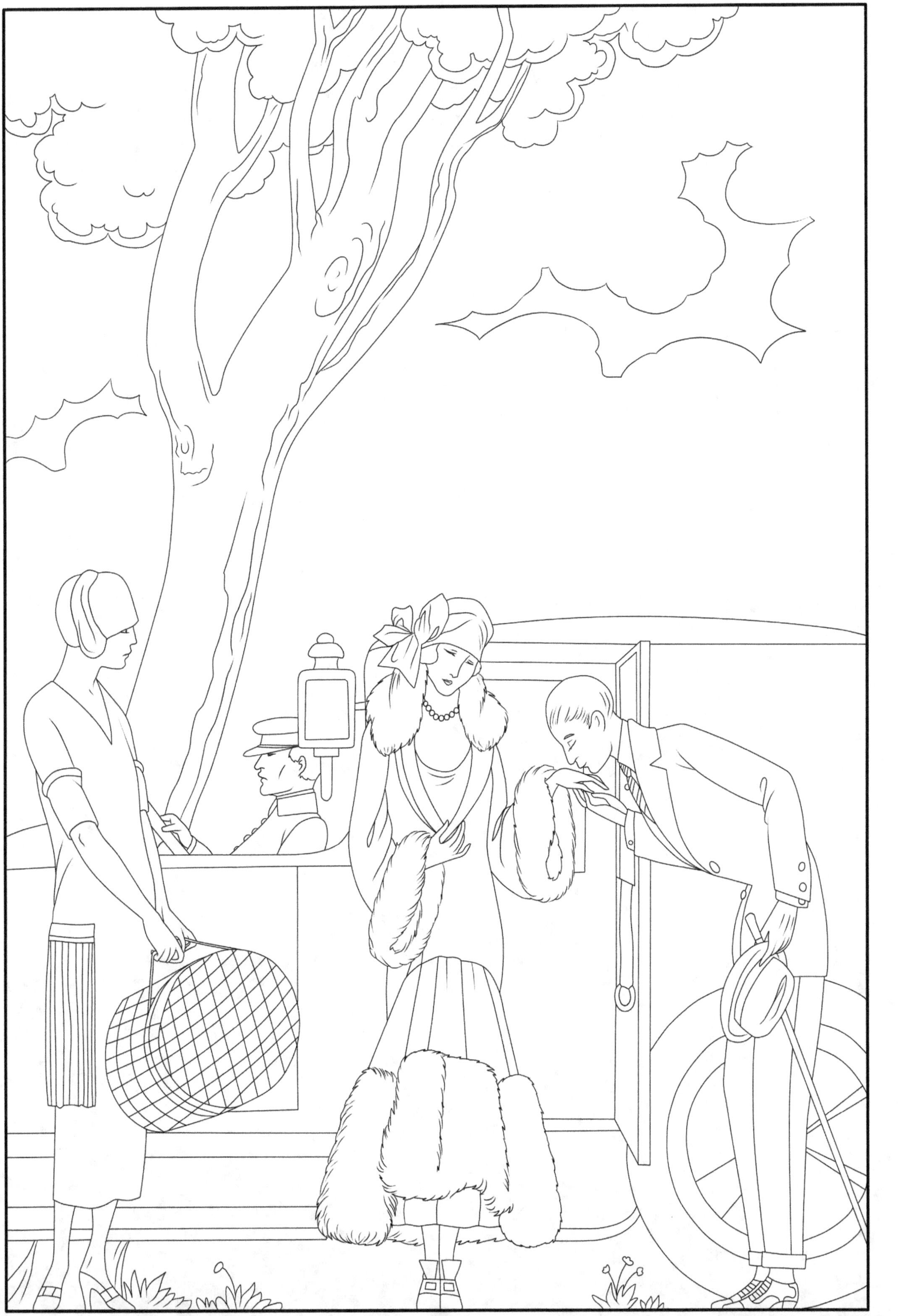

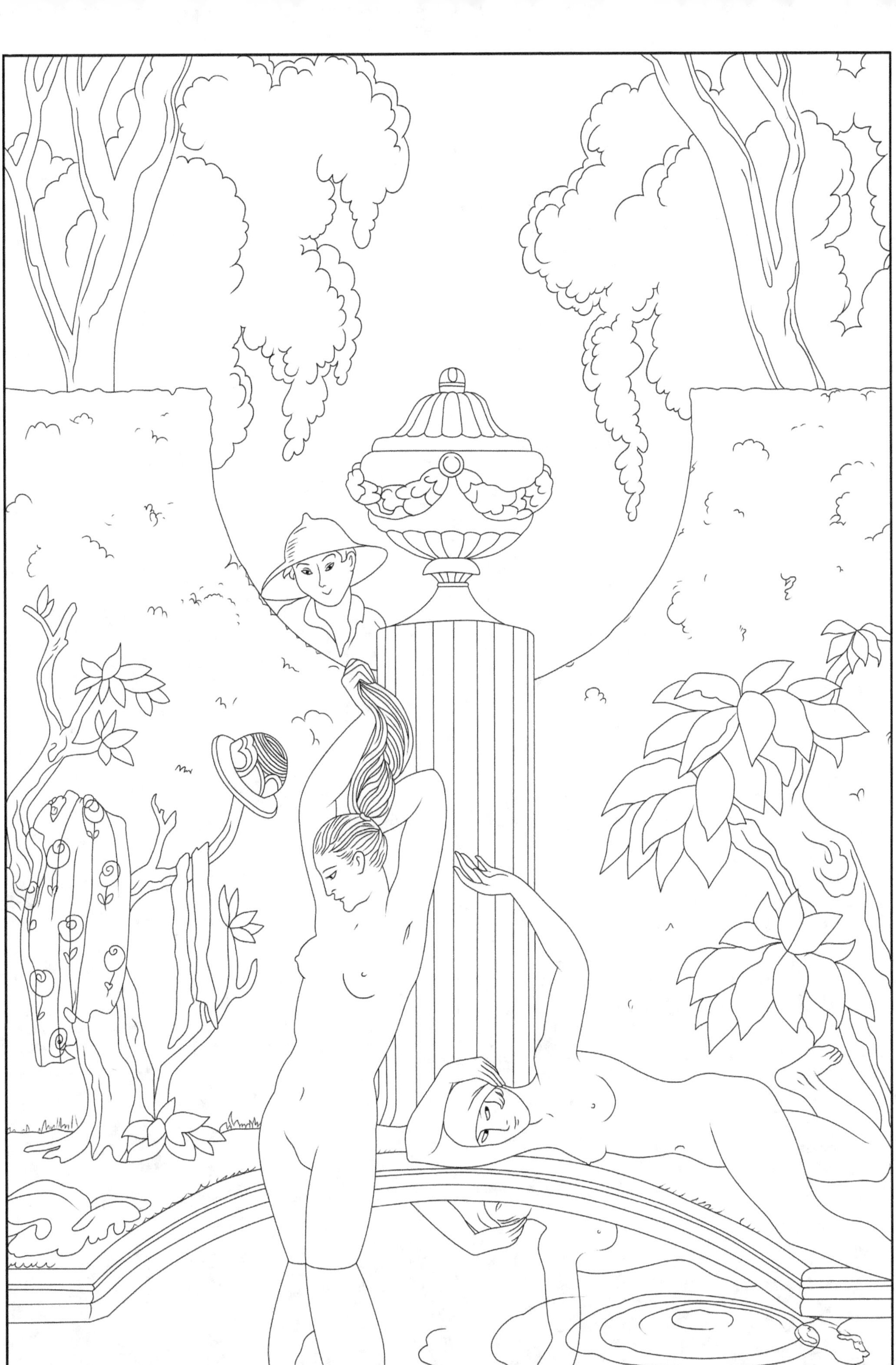

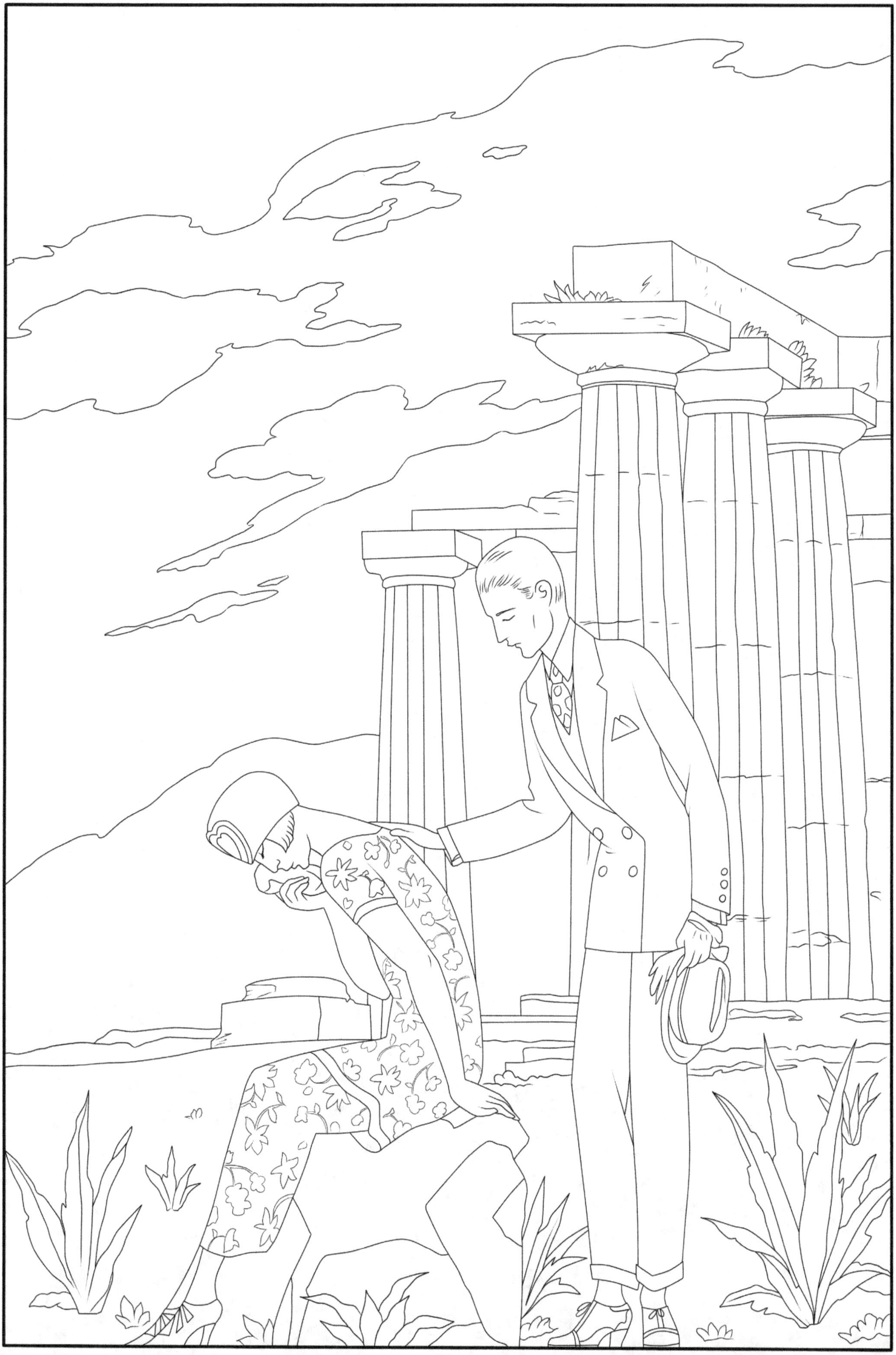

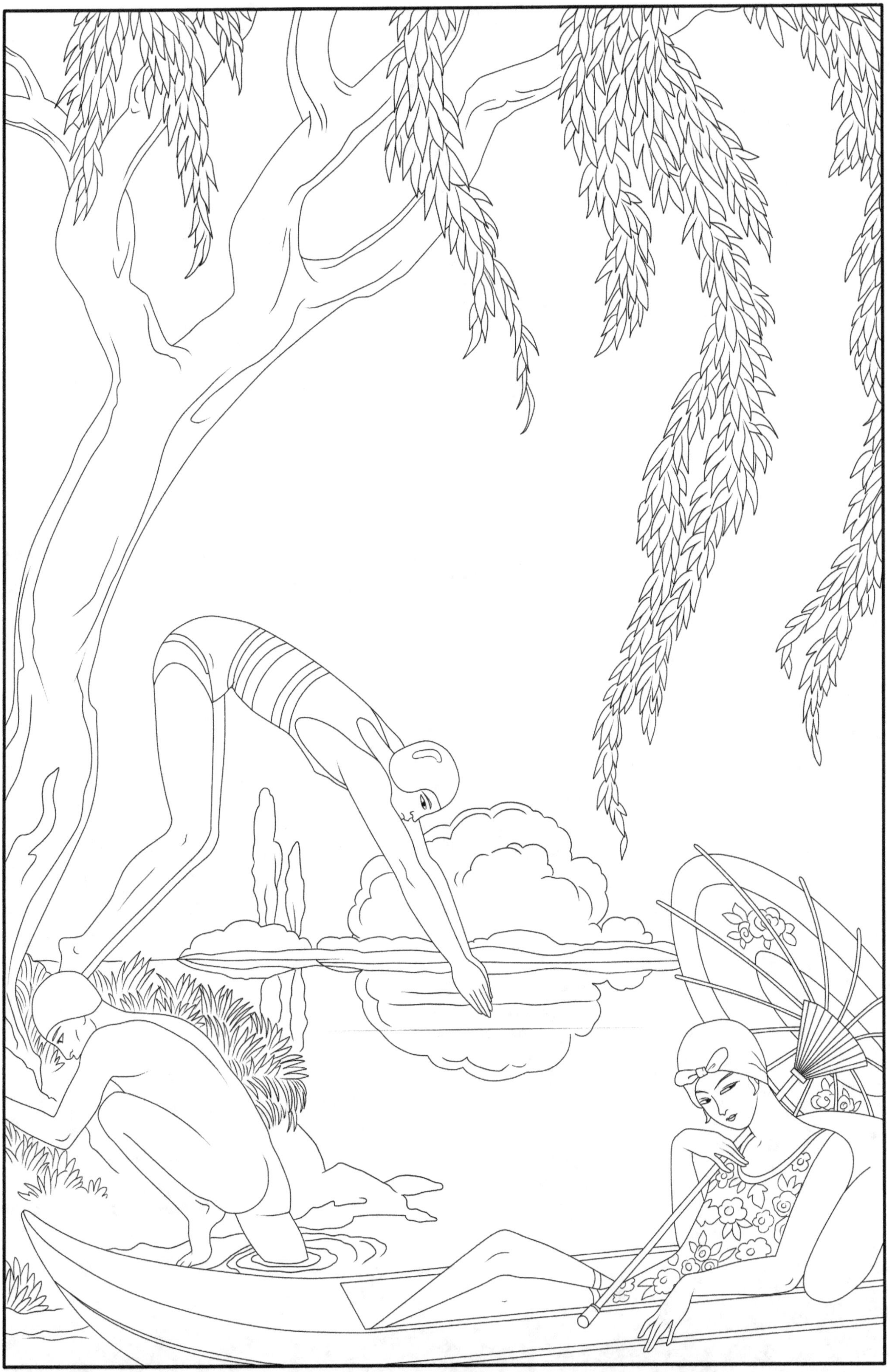

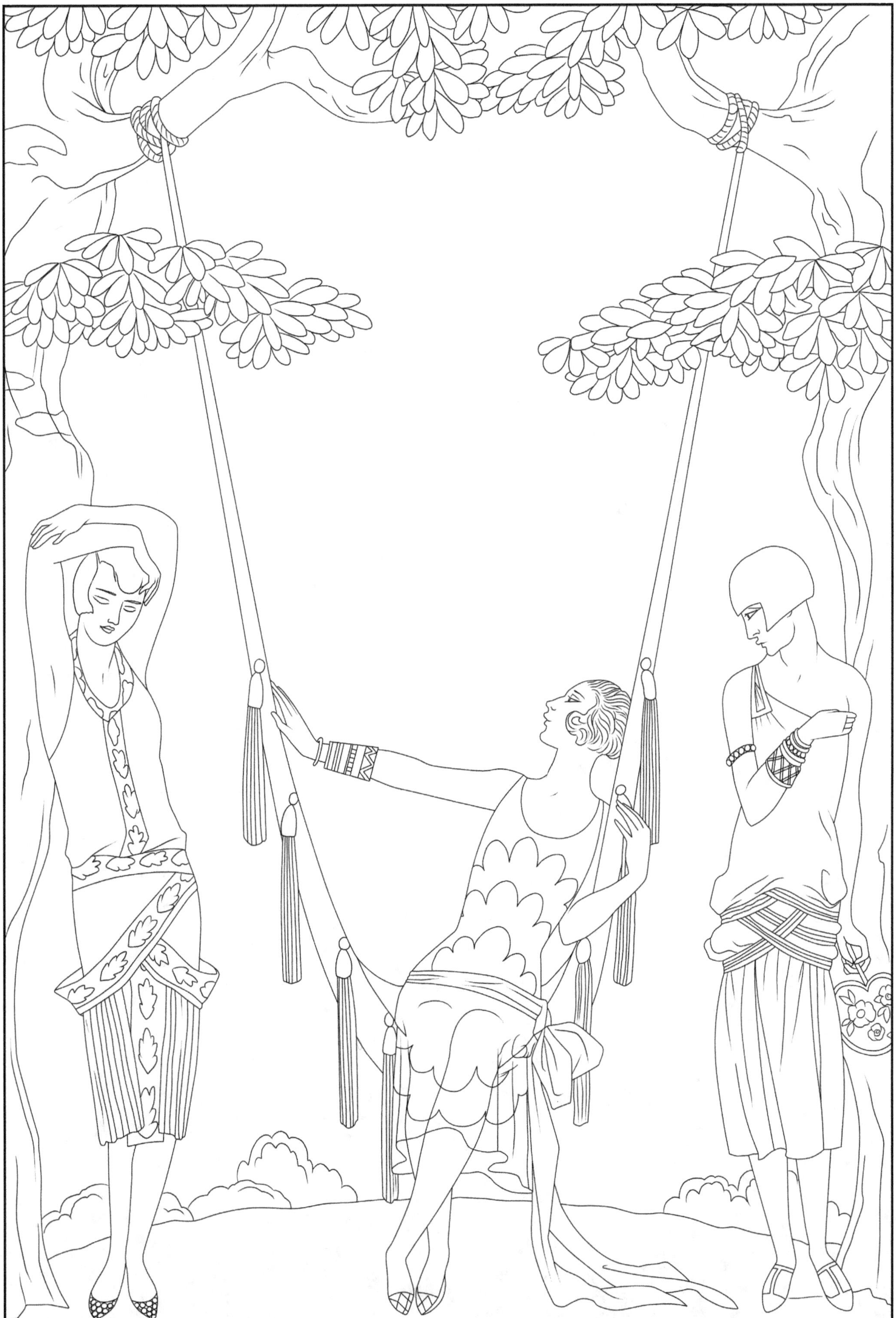

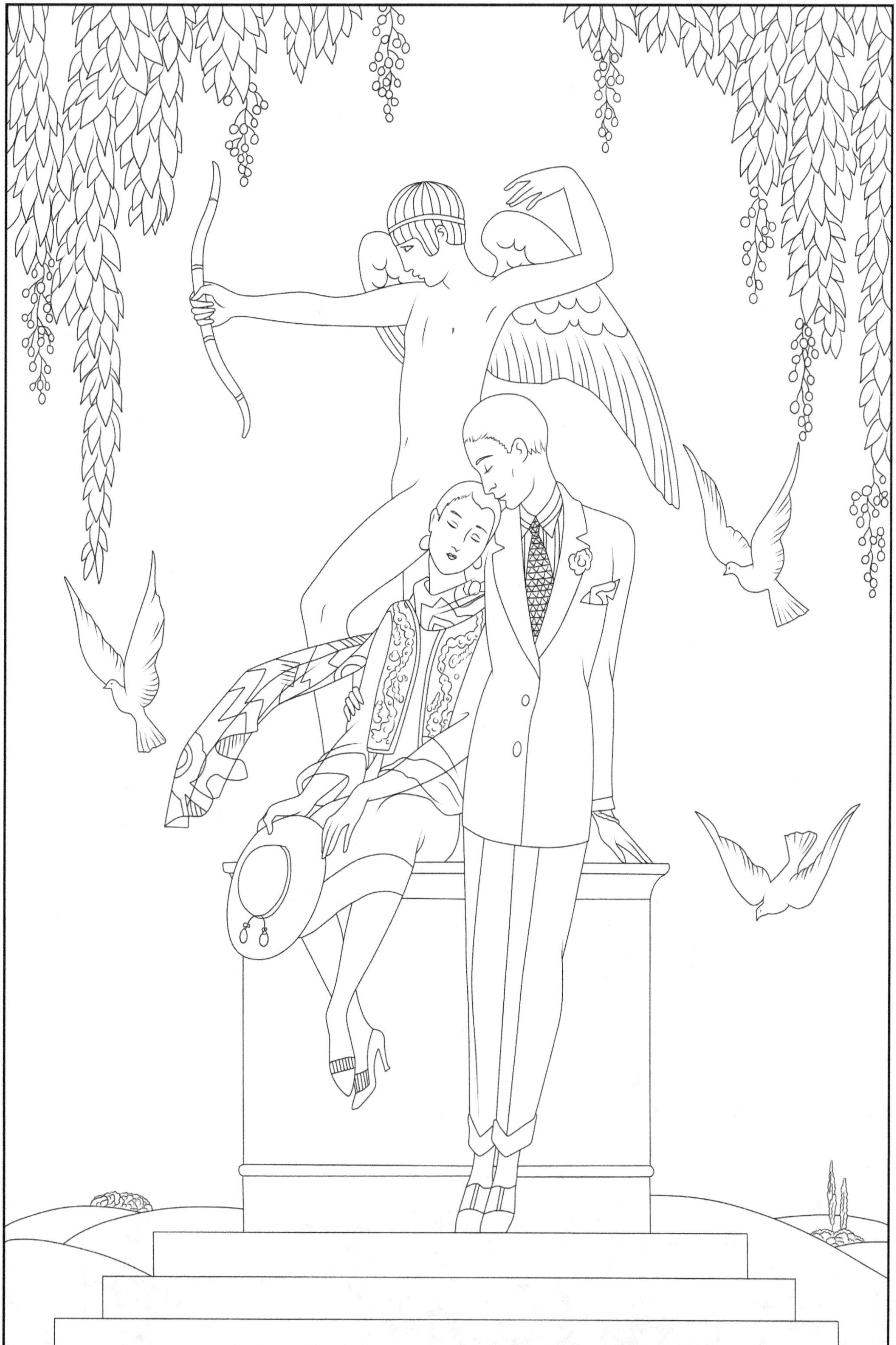

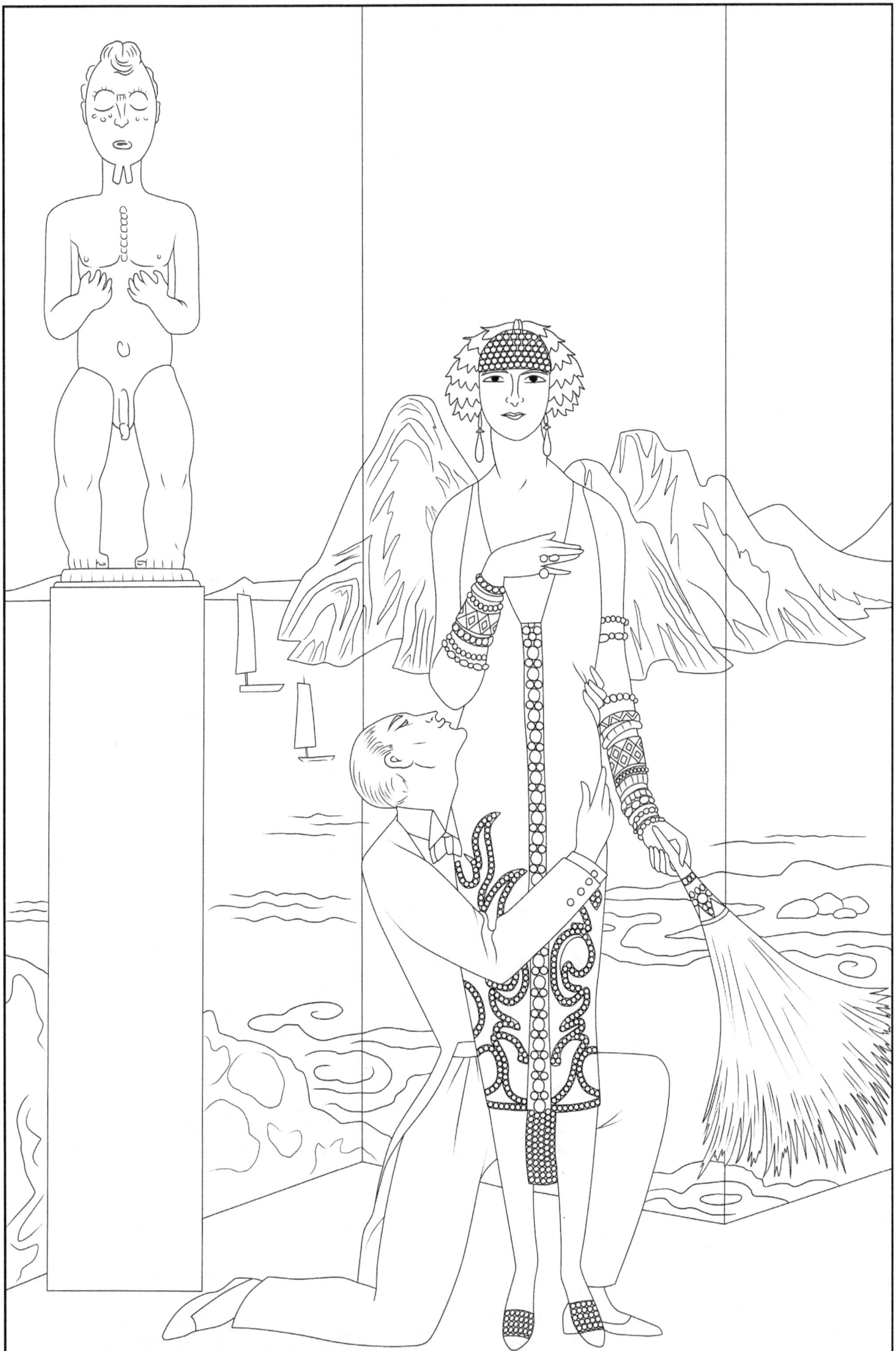

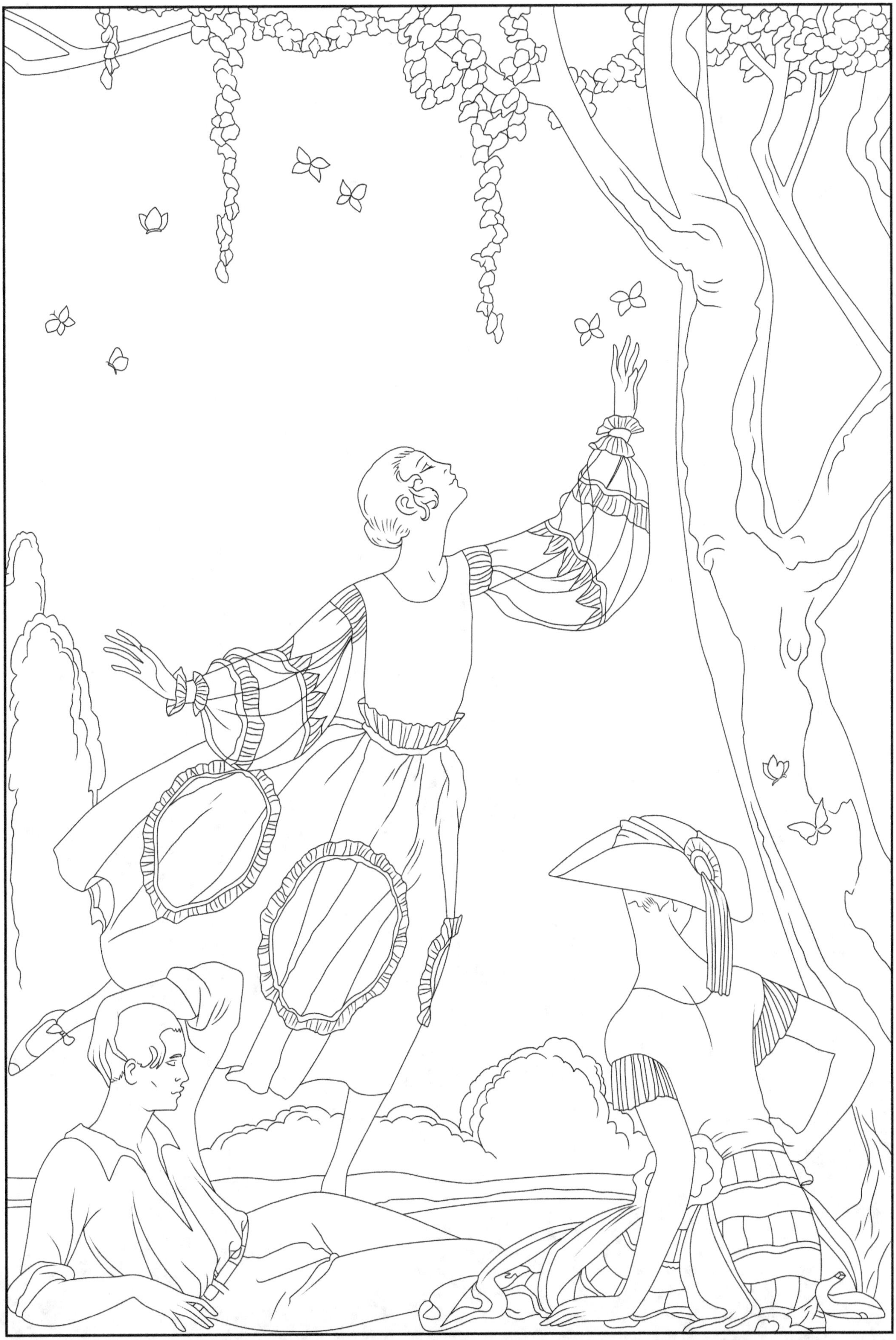

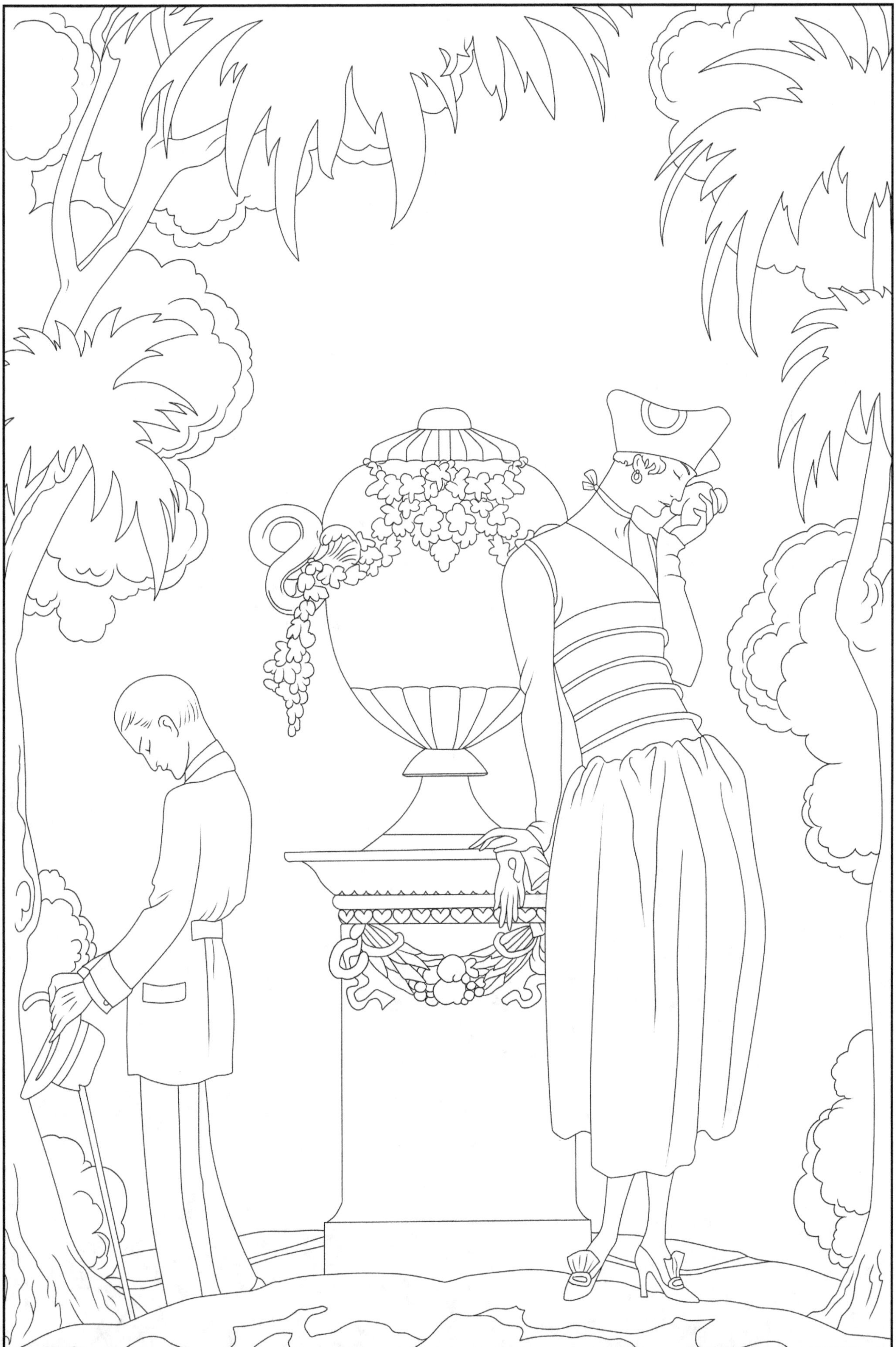

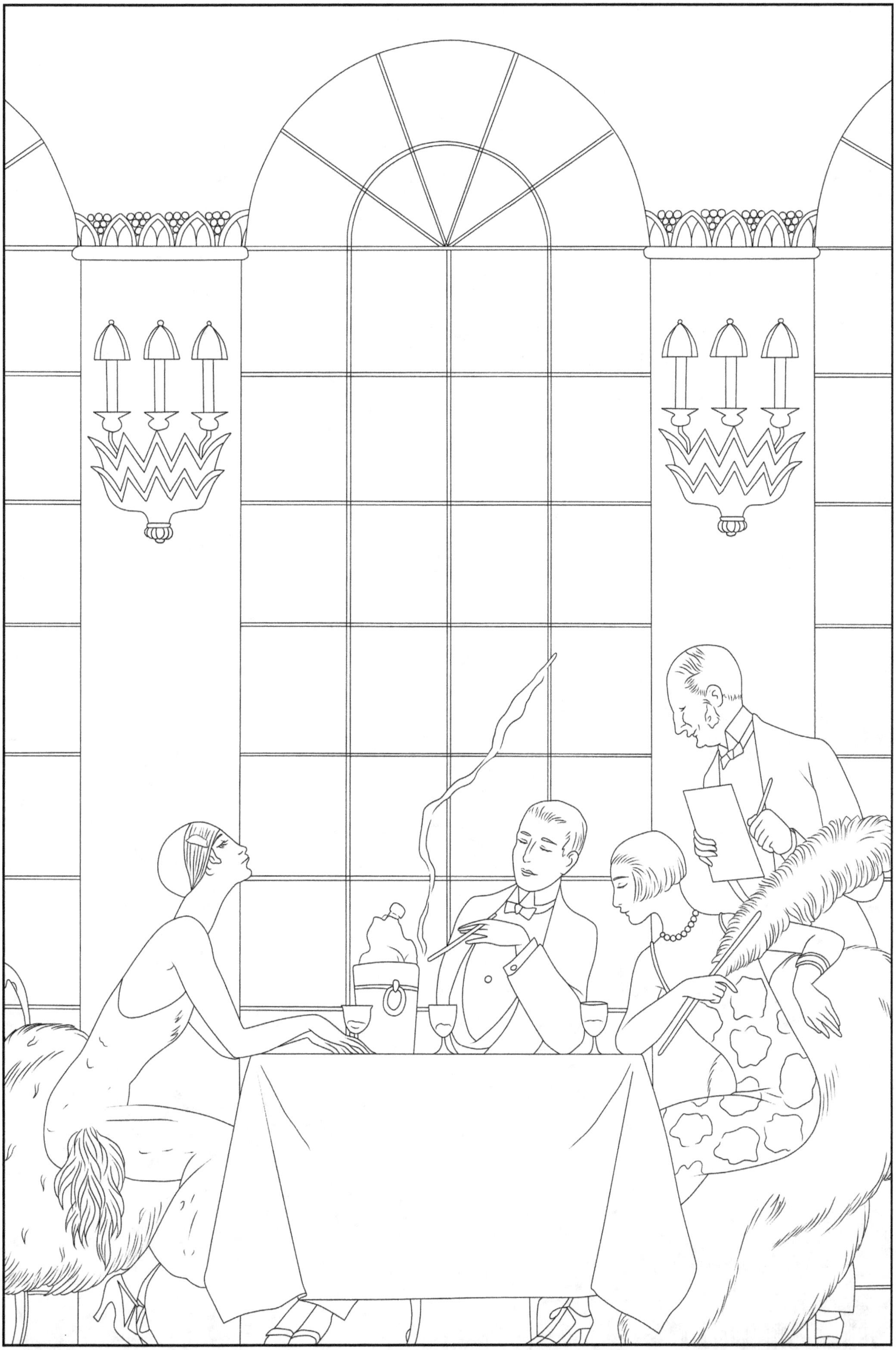

www.ingramcontent.com/pod-product-compliance
Lightning Source LLC
Chambersburg PA
CBHW081621220526
45468CB00010B/2981